10848284

The

LITTLE
BOOK

of

ALPACA
PHILOSOPHY

The

LITTLE

BOOK

of

ALPACA

PHILOSOPHY

A calmer, wiser,
fuzzier way of life

Jennifer McCartney

HarperCollins*Publishers*

'Never be in a hurry; do everything quietly and in a calm spirit. Do not lose your inner peace for anything whatsoever, even if your whole world seems upset.'

Saint Francis de Sales

Contents

Giving thanks for the ability to cross my legs in
such an adorable manner.

Part One
Alpaca the Bags, You Start the Car. Your Journey to a Better Life Begins Now

Alpacas love the journey. There's nothing more fun
than being on the way to somewhere else.

Introduction: Welcome to the Alpaca Philosophy

'Life goes by fast. Enjoy it. Calm down.
It's all funny. Next. Everyone gets so upset
about the wrong things.'

Joan Rivers

The world is a busy place. There's lots of stuff going on that we all care about – the climate crisis, getting good grades and good jobs, washing behind our ears.

In a world of serious overachievers, opinion-havers, Insta-posters and posers with must-read hot takes and commentary on everything and everyone, it can be tough to be a person who likes to just chill and observe. It feels like you're not accomplishing much. You're not contributing to the cacophony, taking a

Remaining zen on public transport.
We can all aspire to this.

stand or standing out. And you're certainly not building an audience. Or a brand. Or whatever else it is we're all supposed to be doing in order to be successful these days. Because the plugged-in people, the ones with the most opinions, are held in the highest regard – look how much they post, contribute, succeed! And we're socialised to try and keep up with all the noise, lest we appear uninformed, uncaring or simply uncool.

But there are loads of us out there – people who prefer to read up, make plans, have lengthy, face-to-face discussions, rather than brief online interactions. People who like to consider all the angles, other people's feelings, the past – and what that means for the future. People who prefer to move a bit more slowly and considerately through the world – or would like to. People who prefer conversations to declarations, long walks to short sprints and the whole bottle rather than just a quick glass. People who prefer the book to the movie (the longer the book, the better). People who don't mind unplugging and taking a walk, once in a while; who always want the full story and thoughtful analysis; and who always seem a little bit chill, unflappable. Those who don't mind a bit of a grey area or some nuance; the ones who want to rise above the fray, just a little bit, and take the long view. *These* are the alpaca people: the ones who stand a little bit apart from the madness. And we can learn a lot from them.

Luckily, the alpaca philosophy is here to teach us. It is the secret to living a better, deeper, more fulfilling life. Or at least to chilling out – just a tiny bit.

Why alpacas? Because alpacas are the best, most resilient and most interesting animals on the planet. More contemplative than the relaxed sloth, more discerning than the playful otter, the alpaca is like the Dalai Llama★ of animals. Until now, they've taken a back seat to more flashy creatures (looking at you, nonsensical unicorn), but *The Little Book of Alpaca Philosophy* seeks to change all that, and introduce these incredible animals – and their wisdom – to the world at large.

Generally, the alpaca is erudite and kind. A bit of an individual (meaning a tad weird). Observant and

★   Just don't call them llamas. Actual llamas are a bit rude.

mellow. It lives a domesticated life of quiet contemplation high in the mountains of South America. A life of reflection. Empathy. Gentle interactions with its fellow herd members. Alpacas are also big on using body language to communicate, which means they're not online a lot. And they've been domesticated for thousands of years, so they're used to getting along with one another, coexisting peacefully with other alpacas and humans alike. They're also neat and organised (helpful when you're living with others) and they're easily trained – as long as you've got food as a reward. They've also got great hair. What better role model is there?

On this reading journey (light walking shoes required, and perhaps a thin jacket – nothing too strenuous involved here) you'll learn some alpaca science and the benefits of serving others (spitting on others, too, on rare occasions), along with quotes, original poetry and quizzes to help you reach a higher plane. With chapters on health and happiness, love and friendship, leisure and pleasure, work and school and home and the universe, you'll learn how best to incorporate the alpaca philosophy into every aspect of your life. Learn the value of watching and waiting, of observation, analysis, meditation and empathy, as opposed to frantic flailing. Plus, the CLIMB method offers a quick and easy way to help you rise above it all.

The alpaca philosophy is urgently needed today. It will resonate with anyone who's longing to expand their outlook, all those who are desperate for a deeper, more reflective and less urgent life and everyone who is searching for a kinder, more loving existence. And, of course, alpacas are very fuzzy. So the alpaca philosophy is also about softening our edges, embracing empathy, kindness and woollen jumpers. Because who can feel overwhelmed or upset while wearing a woolly jumper?

These furry little fuzz units have a lot to teach us – so read on to learn how the alpaca philosophy can help you find a bit of peace and perspective in an overpowering world. Come and hang with the herd. They've been waiting for you. Let's rejoice in the wisdom of these weird little mountain camels!

'Won't you join me?' Alpacas are always welcoming
to others they meet along the way.

Follow the CLIMB Method for a Calmer and Wiser Life

'Generally, we're all doing the best we can. We are not privy to the stories behind people's actions, so we should be patient with others and suspend our judgment of them, recognising the limits of our understanding.'

Epictetus

Learning to live life with an alpaca outlook has a lot of benefits, as you'll soon discover. The joys of being a little bit domesticated (and a little bit wild), while also being generally kind and understanding, will help you put your life in perspective, giving you some peace in an overwhelming world. The CLIMB method is the best and easiest way to remember all

Even our bottoms are adorable.

the main tenets of the alpaca philosophy (especially if the sheer length of this book is, in itself, overwhelming for you!). So fear not. Read on to discover how CLIMB will help you to achieve some balance in all areas of your life. It will also help you to hate humanity a little less. Hopefully.

C

Check out. ★ This key step in the alpaca philosophy is about gaining perspective. The kind that only a bit of time can bring. It's not about giving up or checking out for good. It's about giving yourself permission to not react right away. It's about stepping back,

---

★ Checking out can also refer to library books. Everyone should check out a few library books once in a while – because libraries are one of the world's greatest and most astonishing establishments. Free public institutions dedicated to preserving and providing knowledge to every citizen, regardless of income. Neat!

allowing yourself some time to calm down and figure out a game plan and then returning to the issue with a more balanced viewpoint. You've heard the advice about not sending that email when you're angry? It's because often, when you come back to that same email the next day, whatever it was that made you mad isn't quite so clear any more. In fact, the email you'd write the next day can look very different and is often much more productive than the one you wanted to send in anger. The idea is to avoid putting anger and careless words out into the world if you possibly can.

L

Log out and let it go. This is another version of the above step. But whereas checking out usually involves checking back in at some point to deal with something that needs addressing, logging out and letting go is about, well, exactly that. Take a step back. Log out of your email or social media accounts for a few

hours or a few days – whatever you feel you need.
And rejoin the non-virtual world. Make a cup of tea.
Trim your nails. Look at a bird. Remember what it's
like to be a person occupying and existing within a
physical space. Think about what's important to you
and what's worth your time and energy. And if things
are not worth either of those resources, then let them
all go. Let go of anything that doesn't need your
attention. Everything that doesn't need a response
from you; and whatever can be ignored, whatever
won't matter in an hour, a day, a year, on your death-
bed. The online stuff. The work stuff. The slights and
current events that need your urgent point of view
(they don't).

I

Imagine it the other way around. This step is a
great empathy builder. It's also another way of saying
don't judge until you've walked a mile in another
person's shoes/hooves. It's tough being a person. It's

You're muddling along wonderfully, friend. If it helps just remember that life is fleeting, but also beautiful.

probably tough for that other person to be a person, too. We're all trying to get by. We're all muddling along, struggling to pay bills, fall in love and stay in love, get a job and keep a job. We're all complicated, mixed-up people with lots of weird bits of emotions, contradictory thoughts and unique points of view floating around inside us. So next time you're feeling upset at someone else's actions, take a minute to

15

wonder what they may have been thinking. If at all possible, assume they were acting with good intentions. Maybe you can even take the view that they are just a little bit ignorant – many people are. And, if possible, assume that it's all good and it's not your job to put it right. Let go of your need to correct, chastise, call out or take on the responsibility for educating people whose minds are likely already made up. Acknowledge that other people feel differently from you, and that's ok. Infuriating, but ok.

M

Meet halfway. This is both literal and figurative. If you're meeting someone for drinks or a dinner, always pick a spot in the middle. It's the nice thing to do and it means you're both making an equal effort to get there. This also applies to arguments, discussions, disagreements, apologies. Try and see the other person's point of view and acknowledge it. Generally, don't be an utter cock about stuff. One of the first things we learn about when we're little is the importance of compromise. This step is about acknowledging that this is just as important for us as adults, too.

B

Be kind. This is self-explanatory. There's a reason why we're so desperate for videos of strangers doing nice things for one another. Oh, look, someone helped that lady across the street when she was confused! Oh, look, someone bought that man a pair of shoes when he was in need! And while posting videos of good deeds is a bit of a show-off thing to do, their popularity proves that we all feel pretty happy when other people are nice to each other and to us – and when we're nice to other people, too. Obviously, some people who were raised in barns (rather than in the civilised peaks of the Andes) are very rude and that sucks a lot, but it's part of life. Anyway, the more people choosing to be kind the better. And it starts with you.

Quiz

Determine Your Current Animal Personality

When a unique landmark you visited once is on fire, your immediate thought is:

A. I must find and post a photo of myself in front of this monument, along with a note about how sad I am.

B. I must post an article explaining why everyone posting about how sad they are is actually uncaring because they haven't also posted about another terrible thing that happened recently.

C. What horrible news for humanity and the arts in general. I don't know much about that place, actually, even though I enjoyed visiting it. I wonder what the building was made of? I wonder what its history is? I wonder if they will rebuild it? Look forward to learning more.

D. LOL doesn't affect me. Some old thing on fire. Things burn down all the time. People are too sensitive these days.

E. Everything good is destroyed eventually – what's the point of life?

What an interesting perspective, bird friend.
I hadn't thought of it that way before.

Answers

A: More of a peacock than an alpaca. You're quick to make things about you (which is how we're encouraged to be these days; it isn't all your fault). And while you've got the best of intentions, sometimes it's ok to take the long view: step back and think about how you fit into the bigger picture, if at all. You probably don't fit into it. And that's ok, too.

B: A bit of a badger. It's tough to sit back and watch while people focus all their attention on one sort of generally insignificant thing while other really horrific things are happening the world over. And it's hard not to point out the hypocrisy (and there is definitely a time and place for that). But try stepping back and allowing others their grief, no matter how misplaced you might feel it to be. Donate to a good cause instead of chastising everyone about how they're doing life wrong. Or, if you must engage, try framing your arguments in a way that makes space for duality. We can all be sad about many things at once.

C: You've got a pretty good alpaca outlook. You can acknowledge your feelings without placing yourself at the centre of the issue or minimising other people's thoughts about it. You see big events as an opportunity to learn. When something happens, you're keen to see the bigger picture.

D: A bit of a mole person. Remember than no person is an island (or a mole for that matter). We're all connected to everything in this world and it's ok to feel a personal sense of loss when humanity suffers one. It's also ok to understand that people may feel sad about things you think are silly. Try a bit of empathy next time; perhaps someone got married at that place that's gone now, or visited that spot with their mum, who's since passed away. Everyone's got their reasons for feeling the way they do. Part of developing an alpaca attitude is learning to accept that we are all full of lots of different, contrasting bits.

E: A fainting goat. The world is overwhelming sometimes, and it's good to grieve our losses, both big and small. Feeling things deeply is a beautiful thing, but it can be helpful to keep things in perspective, too. Otherwise it's a bit debilitating. Not everything requires a massive outpouring of emotion. Have a good cry if you must, then move on to something else. Better yet, learn to rise above the fray a little bit. Which is where the CLIMB method comes in.

Part Two
A Practical Guide

Quietly tending to the beautiful living
things in our lives.

Health and Happiness

'Keep calm and carry on.'

Poster produced by the British government during
WWII

'Silence is a source of great strength.'

Lao Tzu

Alpaca Fact: Alpacas flourish in the high,
quiet mountains of the Andes. Their natural habitat
is found at elevations of up to 16,000 feet or
4,800 metres.

Mountain ranges are some of the most peaceful and quiet places on the planet. The Basin and Range mountain region in Oregon and Utah has been found to be one of the quietest places in the US, for example, while the border region between England and Scotland ranks as one of the most tranquil in the UK. There are no high-rises, humming power lines, sounds of industry or commerce. No blaring music or angry shouts. Just the sounds of fuzzy alpacas or caribou or red squirrels nibbling vegetation, accompanied by a bit of wind or birdsong. Sounds nice, doesn't it?

Alpacas thrive in the peace and quiet. And so do we. A study in Dresden, Germany, shows that just two hours of silence creates new cells in the area of the brain linked to emotion, learning and memory. Silence is also thought to lower blood pressure and boost the immune system. A study in *Heart* (the straightforwardly named journal for cardiologists), intended to examine the relaxing effects of music, actually found the participants were most relaxed *in the pauses between the music*. Wild! So while some people seem to thrive on chaos, noise and the big city, take heart that being a person who loves the quiet is just fine as well. In fact, it's good for you.

Alpaca Fact: Around 98 per cent of the world's alpacas were killed during the Spanish conquest of the Aztec Empire in the 1500s.

'Part of the happiness of life consists not in fighting battles, but in avoiding them. A masterly retreat is in itself a victory.'

Norman Vincent Peale

Alpacas have been through some tough times and endured many hardships – including the near extinction of their species at the hands of colonial invaders. But it's kind of cool to think that the 2 per cent of alpacas who survived the wars are the ancestors of every alpaca alive today. Which means every alpaca alive today had a very hardy badass relative who ran for the highest mountain peaks at the first sign of trouble. Well done, alpacas of the past! There are two lessons here.

First, sometimes the best way to persevere, survive, live to fight another day [insert inspirational words of your choice here] is to retreat. Hide out a bit. Take a step back. Withdrawing from the world can be a form of self-preservation and it's nothing to feel ashamed about – it's often a sign of strength. This is especially important to remember today, when there are so many things you may feel passionate about. You may feel obligated to get involved, put yourself out there or to take a stand when it may be better for your mental health or your long-terms goals to move away a little. It's tough when it feels like the universe doesn't reward people for being chill or taking the long view. We're expected to be front and centre of every issue – but at what cost? More and more, everyday people (and celebrities, too) are demonstrating the tenets of the CLIMB method. Log off and let go. Be kind. By giving yourself space to recover and regroup, you'll live to fight another day.

Taking some time off to knit a scarf. Something to keep me warm at the next labour march.

The second lesson is about resilience. Alpaca history encompasses some terrible injustices. Some jerk took one look at an adorable alpaca and decided, 'This offends me'. They decided to do the alpaca harm. Yet, some savvy alpacas took off to the mountaintops and got the last laugh. Biding their time, they got on with life, waiting for the world to recognise their worth. Today, they're thriving. They're one of the most popular animals on the planet. They've even become Instagram famous. And, most importantly, they're still gentle and lovely animals, despite their tragic history.

Generational trauma is real and very difficult to overcome, but it is possible. The alpaca philosophy is about acknowledging difficult aspects of our history, processing it, dealing with it and holding space for the trauma in a way that allows us to continue to live and be alive and light. A good therapist can help with this. And some wonderful day, not too far off from this one, when you remember you've survived and flourished, you can give a little victory dance to celebrate your resilience. You did it! Time to come down from the mountaintop and rejoin the world.

Alpaca Fact: Alpacas eat mostly grass but will occasionally chomp on bark and leaves. They've evolved to avoid things like potatoes, lilies, acorns, walnuts and bracken ferns, which are poisonous to them. Alpacas trust their guts.

'There is a wisdom in this beyond the rules of physic: a man's own observation what he finds good of and what he finds hurt of is the best physic to preserve health.'

Francis Bacon

There's a reason your diet is one of the first things a doctor will ask you about if you're feeling ill. How's your appetite? Have you been eating anything differently over the last few days?

What we eat is key to our health and well-being – and every one of us has different needs. For example, I tried taking multivitamins and discovered they make me extremely tired. There's no scientific evidence that this is a thing. And believe me, I looked. But the fact is, after a few tries I realised, nevertheless, that this was true for me. I stopped taking them and the tiredness went away. Who knows why? Similarly, a friend of mine who was vegan for about ten years was exhausted all the time, had digestion issues and, as a result of this, went on a number of medications over the years, with no significant results. As a last resort, with the support of her medical team, she finally went off her vegan diet and her symptoms disappeared. Weird little anomalies like these are true for all of us. And the alpaca way is about observing what works for us. Noting what makes us feel better or worse. Examining the results. And acting accordingly. With a wealth of information at our fingertips, it's easy to get bogged down in advice, possibilities, diagnoses and suggested treatments. But look inwards first. Trust your body and your brain. All those billions of bacteria and electricity and energy that make up who you are – they know you best. Listen to them.★ They're probably telling you they don't like gluten.

> **Alpaca Fact:** All baby alpacas are known as 'crias'; but if we wanted to be more specific, a baby female is a 'hembra' and a male is a 'macho'.

Animals can't tell us how they feel about the sex they're assigned at birth. Hopefully, they feel ok about

---

★ Also listen to your doctor. There's a reason why hundreds and thousands of years of science exist, and that's to help you. Basically, every scientific thing that's ever been investigated since the beginning of time has been part of a quest to help humankind in some way (or make some greedy patent holder a bunch of money; two sides to everything, really). So eat your herbal sandwiches, but also take your life-saving insulin and give thanks to Frederick Banting, James Collip and Charles Best who sold the insulin patent to the University of Toronto for a dollar, so that everyone around the world could use this drug as needed at a very low cost.

it. The gender norms of animals are pretty loosey-goosey anyway. Pink tutus or monster-truck onesies are never foisted upon unsuspecting baby alpacas by their well-meaning parents. Luckily, as human beings, we can identify and express our gender in whichever way feels good and right to us. We also love who we love and that's also cool. The alpaca philosophy is all about that inner journey – observing your thoughts and feelings closely and being true to all that, no matter your age or situation in life. An alpaca person takes the time to figure out what feels right and true, and then does that thing, generally in a chill, confident way. Because there's nothing more liberating than being you.

Alpaca Fact: There are two alpaca breeds: the suri and the huacaya. The suri have long, wavy hair, while the huacaya have fluffy, teddy-bear hair. Both are equally adorable.

A very content group of alpaca friends,
living their best lives.

Looking good, sweetheart. Yes, you.
You're very loved.

The alpaca philosophy is all about self-love. And learning to love the way you look is an important part of being alive. Alpacas, for example, know that fluffy, teddy-bear hair and wavy, silky locks are both fab. They're also perfectly content when it's all shaved off. And we can learn from this. Dyed, shaved, permed or straightened, thinning or thick – under all that skin and hair our souls are all the same. And if you're struggling a bit with self-acceptance,* take comfort from knowing that no matter what style you're rocking today, 20 years from now, you'll 100 per cent look back at old photos and wonder what on earth you were thinking. That's just universal.

---

* Like those headachy mornings after a night of glitchpop and energy drinks, when you really question your life choices? Those nights are worth it. It's ok to look and feel like crap in the morning.

This alpaca comes with a warning.
Does not play nice with others.

> **Alpaca Fact:** Male alpacas can suffer from something inventively called Berserk Male Syndrome. This occurs when they are raised in isolation by humans and become overly aggressive with their handlers; it manifests as biting, charging, chest ramming and even what are known as 'sneak attacks'. The syndrome can be prevented by castration.

As well-mannered and generally chill as alpacas can be, they can occasionally lose it. This sometimes calls for understanding and better training, but sometimes it requires the alpacas to be put down. That's life. Go too far and pay the price. The lesson here is: violence has consequences. And no matter how cute an animal or person appears to be at first glance, once you've experienced these violent tendencies, it's best to stay away.

If you happen to be already involved with or living with someone who is violent towards you (one in three women and one in four men reports being the

victim of violence at the hands of an intimate partner), know that while this is unfortunately very
common, it is also not acceptable. When you are
ready, there is always a way out.★ You've got options
– friends, helplines, safe spaces and entire communities (both online and in real life) waiting to lend an
ear or a hand. And remember, the best predictor of
future behaviour is past behaviour. An alpaca said that
once. Or maybe it was Mark Twain. No one seems to
know for sure.

Alpaca Fact: Alpaca history spans millions of years
and many continents.

Taking the long view can be very difficult these days.
News is immediate and bite-size. Everything is a
reaction to everything else, and it's all urgent, panicked
and confusing. It's rare we get to experience a
nuanced, long read – something that takes into

★   Not castration.

account the history of a thing. The best we can do is to be aware of our potentially myopic viewpoints and put a bit of effort into learning some stuff. Books are a good place to start. Colonialism, slavery, genocide, famine, wars, pandemics (along with medical break-throughs), great works of art, agriculture – all those things that took place over centuries shaped who we are and how we live today. Don't believe it? Do you live in a castle and have millions of pounds? No? Well, the lucky people who do, and who eat fancy things out of heirloom dishes served by butlers, have their ancestors from hundreds of years ago to thank for their current situation. Anyway, the alpaca philosophy is about embracing the long view and knowing it gives us a better, more nuanced understanding of everything we experience today.* This practice often offers us a sense of peace and perspective. Stuff's been happening for millions of years. It will continue to happen long after we go.

---

* The alpaca philosophy also acknowledges life is definitely not fair.

Alpaca Fact: Alpacas can become depressed if isolated from the herd.

In a world that seems to worship individualism, going it alone and forging one's own path, it's important to remember that we're all social creatures that need one another, just like alpacas. There's a reason why domesticated alpacas are raised in herds. Herds are very nice. They involve cooperation (everyone gets their own bit of grass and uses the same toilet) and tolerance ('Hortense the Alpaca is just so bossy, isn't she? However, she is dealing with that thing with her sister. She's been sort of upset about that lately.'*) Needing people is ok. It's not a weakness; it's how we were designed.

But while we may know that togetherness is good for us, it's not always an option. A survey by the Campaign to End Loneliness found that 9 million UK residents have reported feeling lonely. And just

---

* An alpaca demonstrating tolerance, somewhere, probably.

What kind of tea do alpacas love?
Any kind, as long as it's shared with friends
on a lovely stripey blanket.

like alpacas, lonely humans can become depressed. This isn't a problem with an easy solution. But there are small steps you can take to mitigate its effects. One thing the campaign suggests is to celebrate the small moments of connection we have day to day. Stuff like saying hello to someone in the shops or smiling at someone on the street. Chatting with the postman about the weather or having a video catch-up with someone you don't see very often. These small efforts go a long way. So if you're living alone, or simply feeling a bit lonely, aim for a small bit of kinship whenever you can. And if you're lucky enough to be feeling particularly connected to your herd these days, keep in mind, as you're bustling around the world, that there are lonely people out there who are counting on you. Stay open to opportunities for connection. Try smiling. Build a bit of love in your own community, one wave or chat at a time.

> **Alpaca Fact:** Alpacas grow to a height of about 3 or
> 4 feet, depending on the breed. Lengthwise they
> can reach about 7 feet.

Alpacas are average-sized animals. Bigger than your
dog, cat or a bunch of chickens. Smaller than a horse,
giraffe or elephant. Bigger than a fox. Smaller than a
whale. You get the idea. Alpacas have evolved to be
just the right size – the size they are. No one looks at
an alpaca and goes, *Oh, if only this were smaller and more
cute!* Or, *Gee, if this thing was bigger it would be so much
more impressive!* That's because we tend to accept
animals for how they are – something we rarely do
when it comes to ourselves. The next time you look
in the mirror and think, I wish my nose was 4 inches
to the left, or, I wish my eyelashes weren't so curly, ask
yourself whether you'd be as critical of an alpaca's
weird little floofy face that looks like the top of a
dandelion gone to seed. Probably not. Because
animals are perfect the way they are. And you are, too.

> **Alpaca Fact:** Alpacas don't need a lot of food to survive compared to other animals their size.

Alpacas don't lend themselves to excess. Although there's nothing wrong with excess, really. We all indulge occasionally. But while no one needs more opinions about food and wellness and which trendy vitamin or superfruit or garlic facial is the best to ward off old age,★ we could usefully apply this take-what-we-need-and-no-more mindset to other areas of our lives. This is especially helpful in an age of billionaires who own private islands, celebrities with 350 handbags, bigger homes and bigger cars and even bigger credit-card debts. More filters and more followers. We want more. We aspire. We spend. We want what we don't have. And what we don't need.

Luckily, you likely already have enough. Maybe even an abundance. Here's a quick checklist:

★   Old age comes for us all, if we're lucky. Embrace it.

- Have you got a pair of shoes?
- A light jacket for rainy weather?
- Do you know what you're having for lunch?
- Is there someone nearby who cares about you?
- Have you got enough toilet paper?
- Do you have a good book to read? Possibly one about animals?
- Can you see a tree or a bit of sky from your window right now?
- Are you still breathing air, pumping blood, existing in the world?

The answer is probably yes to most of the above and, hopefully, definitely yes to the last one. Like the alpaca, you don't need a whole lot to survive. At least not much more than you already have.

A Limerick About Finding Inner Peace

There was an alpaca named Spence,
Who loved to 'just add his two cents',
He soon got blocked
'Cause of how much he talked
Now he's happy, offline, in his tent.

Spence stopped talking and got a healing bit of shut-eye.

Love, Family and Friendship

'True love is not a strong, fiery, impetuous passion. It is, on the contrary, an element calm and deep. It looks beyond mere externals, and is attracted by qualities alone. It is wise and discriminating, and its devotion is real and abiding.'

Ellen G. White

Alpaca Fact: When alpacas sit, they fold their legs under their bodies, forming a neat little alpaca package. You'll never find a manspreading alpaca – they're much too considerate for that.

Being considerate about the amount of space you take up may seem a bit quaint – especially these days, when we (mostly women) are encouraged to make space at the table for ourselves: *take up space! Make your voice heard! Elbow your way in!* But the alpaca philosophy wants us to be aware of our own physical and emotional boundaries. It isn't asking us to make ourselves smaller or less obtrusive to please others at the expense of our own comfort, though. It's about understanding what we're comfortable with, and what others may be comfortable with, too. And acting accordingly – with the understanding that if we're careful with how much space *we* take up, we may be able to create more space for someone else, which is always a nice thing to do. Making room for others is a key tenet of the alpaca philosophy.

Physically, it's a good idea not to take up more space than is generally polite – if you're on public transport, keep your feet off the seats and your bag on the floor or on your lap. If you're driving, stay out of the bike lanes, and if you're parking, do it neatly and considerately. If you're in a relationship, don't sleep starfish-style on the bed. Or, you know, try it on with someone who doesn't want to be tried on with. Emotionally, being aware of the space we take up means leaving room for others to speak once we've said our bit – at the meeting, in an argument, on the campaign trail, on the spaceship (see, being considerate doesn't mean you can't have very important, high-powered jobs). If you prefer cheesy sayings, then this is a good one: in making room for others, we make room for ourselves. An alpaca said that once, probably.

Alpaca Fact: Alpacas love weddings.

Something that people do now is to hire alpacas to hang out at their weddings. Alpacas don't mind and they look great dressed up in little coats and hats. They're happy to pose for pictures and to help make someone's day that much more special. Loving weddings is an important skill to develop. It takes time. Often, when we're young, a wedding invite is a bit of a pain. Financially, it means taking time off work that we can't really afford, travelling somewhere random and buying an annoying present from the registry – like a sassy welcome mat or a subscription to a frying-pan-of-the-month club. Mentally, it can sometimes mean feeling a bit bummed about our own station in life – a crappy relationship or a recent break-up, perhaps. But it may help to remember this: there are very few times in our lives when we have the opportunity to gather with loved ones for the purpose of feeling and expressing joy.

You will attend a limited number of weddings in your lifetime and you won't appreciate how lovely they were until they're over. As you get older, the wedding invites come less often, and then stop altogether. Hello, divorce parties! And someday you'll look at the wedding selfie you took with the friendly alpaca dressed as Jane Austen, and remember fondly the days when you had an excuse to get dressed up, drink champagne with your friends and dance until the wee hours. So say yes to every wedding invite. Show up and take photos. And thank the alpacas for their service.

Alpaca Fact: Alpacas show affection by nose nuzzling. They may even give you a wee kiss if they're very happy. They're not big on hugs.

In a world of over-emoting (16 emojis minimum for every birth announcement, engagement and anniversary), the act of showing affection these days can seem a bit performative. Posting about sibling love on international sibling day feels like a requirement. Not 'loving' photos of babies seems a bit rude. And heaven forbid we don't gush about our relationship on Valentine's Day. These exuberant online displays of affection have become the norm. But according to a study published in the *Personality and Social Psychology Bulletin*, these loved-up posts can, in fact, mask a lot of relationship insecurity: the higher a person's desire for 'relationship visibility', the more anxious about that relationship they may be.

The alpaca philosophy acknowledges that while heartfelt, over-the-top love and excitement can be gorgeous and wonderful things to express (when

I love you even though I didn't post
about it online.

done from a place of happiness and security), some of us prefer to keep our love on the down-low, and that's fine, too. And actually, pretty healthy. Some of us love an in-person hug, a hang out, an exchange of smiles. Some of us like to send our thoughts via snail mail. Some of us are a bit more private when it comes to expressing our feelings – or at least, it seems that way when compared to the stuff we see online. These quieter ways of emoting are often enough, though. Enough to help us receive and express love in a way that feels comfortable. So whether you're a big bear-hug emoter or a nuzzly alpaca type of person, just know there's no wrong way to show you care.

Alpaca Fact: Alpacas can live harmoniously in nature with mountain lions, sheep, coyotes, flamingos, condors and spectacled bears. They also get along well with people.

Living things are all very gentle and require love and affection to thrive. Don't hug the cactus, though.

Have a think about those videos showing a golden retriever and a mallard having a nap together. Or a piglet and a kitten play fighting. Or a panda bear and a baby goat having tea. How adorable those unlikely friendships are when you see them in action. It's sweet, right? Heart-warming. It makes you feel a little more optimistic about humankind. That could be you! All it takes is a little bit of open-mindedness.

Getting along with others who aren't quite like ourselves is a very important part of the alpaca philosophy. It can also be very rewarding. This doesn't mean hanging out with those who are outright mean or who wish us harm. But it does mean keeping an open mind about people we might not normally choose as friends or even want to chat with. Maybe it's someone who believes in UFOs. Or a person who loves to run marathons. Or someone who loves gourmet food, while you're into your auntie's roast potatoes. Maybe it's an older relative with outdated★ views on

---

★   Remember that will be us someday. 'Ugh,' your hip young niece will admonish from her hoverboard. 'Those views are *so* early 21st century.'

technology or politics. Remember the CLIMB method. Be kind. That's how unlikely friendships start.

Alpaca Fact: Alpacas are members of the camelid family. This includes South American llamas, guanacos and vicunas as well as the African and Asian Bactrian and dromedary camels. All of these animals originated in the plains of North America around 10 million years ago. That's right, camels are native to North America. Surprise!

Alpacas are part of a very large family. And yet they all seem to get along. We can learn from this, hopefully. Being part of a family is tough. Our relatives are constantly delighting us and disappointing us, depending on the holiday, group chat or dinner plan. Astonishing us with their thoughtfulness or not-thoughtfulness, with their political views, their capacity for love and for making us upset. Remember the CLIMB method. Let it go. Meet halfway. And be

We both inherited mum's penchant for pom-poms.

kind. We're all very different, no matter how closely we're related, and that's ok.

Alpaca Fact: Alpacas travel in herds.

The word 'herd' has a bit of a negative connotation. It implies a mass of people all doing the same thing, without thinking for themselves. The good news is, herds are also awesome. A herd is 'a social group of animals'. Nothing wrong with that. I mean, alpaca herds hang out looking at mountains, snacking on grass and feeling at one with the universe, probably. Sounds nice, doesn't it?

Imagine hanging out with a group of souls who just get you on a fundamental level and who are with you, no matter what. The alpaca philosophy is about finding your lovely herd – and being ok with being part of a group in a world that seems to value individualism over everything. It might be at the library or in a book club. (Finding people who like the same books as you is a magical discovery. Maybe

I 'herd' you like to cook. Join us!

they also love books about alpacas!) It might be at the BMX track or a hot-yoga class. (Chatting while producing endorphins is a wonderful way to bond with your herd.) It may be after-work cocktails or after-class beers (obviously, lots of alcohol is conducive to bonding). It could be a parenting or a ceramics class. Herds are a source of strength and solidarity. They're also good for your health: research has shown that interacting with others gives us an emotional boost. And socialising can actually reduce our risk for dementia. And, of course – it's nice to feel we belong somewhere.

> **Alpaca Fact:** Male alpacas make an 'orgling' sound to attract a mate. It sounds a bit like a car trying to start. Or like a horse trying to gargle.

The alpaca mating sound is horrible and funny and very hard on the ears. But luckily, lady alpacas don't seem to mind. As a species, alpacas are flourishing all over the planet! Our own attempts at finding love can often feel awkward and a bit silly – we're orgling into the void, wondering who on earth is going to love us with all our quirky bits and annoying habits and special secrets. We can also feel a bit vulnerable. But the good news is everyone else is feeling the same. No matter how many first-person essays on finding love you may read, or how many dating self-help books you may finish, I'll let you in on a little secret: no one knows what they're doing! We're all just out there making weird noises and hoping someone finds that pretty cool. And eventually, you find your person.* That special someone who makes you feel loved and accepted just as you are. Orgling and all.

---

*   Maybe not your forever person, maybe just for a bit. Nothing wrong with that, though. Hopefully, throughout your long life, you'll be lucky enough to connect with various someones who make you feel nice.

Quiz

Find Your Alpaca Love Language

What's your favourite romantic movie?

A. It's a toss-up between *Die Hard* and *Thelma and Louise*. Both so sweet.

B. *Princess Bride*. So weird and lovable!

C. *Into the Wild*. Where the guy finally finds peace and happiness in that old bus.

D. Does *The Office* count? I really like things I've already seen 40 times that I don't have to think about.

When you've got a crush on someone, you tend to:

A. Hire a songwriter, pay for a recording studio and a few musicians, record an album and release it online.

B. Wait for your crush to organically come across the song you've named after them; if that doesn't get their attention, you try skywriting.

C. Make excuses to spend some time with them (Oh! You're about to go sharpen your pencil? What a coincidence? Let me join you at the blackboard.)★

D. Write about them in your screenplay.

What's your favourite way to pass the time?

A. Playing rugby. Ideally in the mud.

B. Brunching with friends. Preferably at a place that has fun wallpaper that looks great in a social media post.

★ That's if you're living in 1986. If it's present day, you tend to just engage with their social media posts.

C. Reading a book by an Italian novelist, while eating a croissant at a café.

D. Watching plants grow.

Your loved one ate your ginger cookies. The ones you got at the shops in the Scottish Highlands. How do you communicate your anger?

A. State your case strongly, using emotional language and 'You ...' statements.

B. Explain what's bothering you and ask them to order you new cookies online.

C. Clam up, walk away and stew silently.

D. Slowly take bites out of *their* favourite thing over the next few weeks, until it's all gone.

Answers

Mostly As: Living that llama life. There's nothing wrong with being a bit forward and letting out a bit of aggression now and then. But the alpaca philosophy is about being a bit less confrontational and a bit more chill. The next time you're tempted to make something all about you and your needs, take a deep breath and remember the CLIMB method. Your partner will thank you.

Mostly Bs: Classic alpaca. Suave, well-balanced, a wee bit quirky and never too showy. You tend to be straightforward and emotionally available when it matters.

Mostly Cs: Chilly penguin. A little cool and a little reserved, sometimes. It's nice to get a bit of perspective, to remove yourself from the hustle and bustle and the petty-seeming concerns of others. But remember, we're all in this together. Communication and openness are essential tools for us herd animals.

Mostly Ds: Sloth love. You like to take things slow, and you're not so obsessed with being productive. What's meant to be will be. Time to check out *The Little Book of Sloth Philosophy* for more tips on how to live that sloth life.

A Note on Parenting

Alpaca Fact: Alpacas give birth in the morning. Around 90 per cent of deliveries occur between 8 am and noon.

Morning births allow the crias to dry off, stumble around a bit in the warm sun and bond with Mum before night falls and temperatures drop. This reduces the chances of the baby getting hypothermia. And no middle-of-the-night labour for Mum – also a bonus.

Alpaca mums, like mums everywhere, have evolved to be extremely smart and good at their jobs. Who wants a cold, wet baby delivered at 3 am? Not alpacas, thank you. They like to plan ways to make their parenting lives easier. For human parents, that kind of self-preservation takes many forms – meal prep, babysitters, fancy poop-tracking baby apps, summer camps, prosecco. Whatever gets you through. The point is, whether we're being raised by a parent, or we're the ones doing the raising, we can all acknowledge there's a lot of effort involved in making a healthy person. And it can also be a bit confusing; nobody really knows what's best. Old-timey parents used to give their babies beer and gin. Doctors thought breastfeeding after nine months gave babies brain damage. Psychologists said showing affection for your kid would lead to a lifetime of disappointment, so they advised against it. Everything we thought we knew was wrong. Which brings us back to the long view of the alpaca philosophy: whatever you're doing is fine. They'll probably turn out ok. Remember to feed them now and then, make sure they're warm and that they're safe and dry at night, and they'll likely grow up to be adorable, well-adjusted things. They won't turn out as cute as an alpaca, though.

Creating healthy things to live on in the world
after you're gone is an admirable way to
spend your lifetime.

> **Alpaca Fact:** Alpacas communicate by humming softly. They also 'wark' when they're excited. Have you ever heard of anything more adorable?

One reason why people love to raise alpacas is because of their absolute chill. No shrieking like chickens or snorting like pigs. No incessant dopey mooing like you'd get from a cow. No tantrums or sulking like toddlers or teenagers. Just a lovely little hum when they're happy.★ It's no wonder people enjoy having them around.

Quiet communication is a bit of a lost art, these days. We're always being told that the louder you talk, the more persuasive you can be and the more confident you seem. Unfortunately, some loud talkers take this to the extreme. We've all been sat next to someone on public transport or at a café or airport who can't seem to use their indoor voice. LISTEN TO HOW IMPORTANT I AM, is how it sounds to the

★   And a few whinnies and guttural noises when they're not.

rest of us. Which is maybe why we also associate loud conversations with annoying, rude and self-centred people. 'The rest of society be damned', they seem to be saying with their loudness. This also applies to people who shout on the internet.

Luckily, though, there are many people who still practise the gentle art of conversation. Who value a measured back and forth at a reasonable volume. Who feel comfortable communicating at an acceptable decibel. Think of all the calming people you know who make a habit out of speaking softly. Psychiatrists. Yoga instructors. Pilots. Massage therapists. Librarians. And the next time you feel like screaming, try a gentle hum instead.

Alpaca Personalities or Big Alpaca Energy (BAE)

There are a ton of celebrities who embody Big Alpaca Energy. Celebrities who, for some reason, everyone seems to be genuinely fond of. Having BAE doesn't mean you have to be likeable or well-mannered. But it means you live your life in such a way that people generally seem to respect you and whatever it is you choose to do. It often means doing things that benefit others and bring joy. Things that make the world a better place. Anyone – from a barista to a kindergarten teacher to a graffiti artist to a furniture restorer to a train operator – can have BAE, but here are some famous examples.

Keanu Reeves
Actor Keanu is a good person, by all accounts. He's never in the tabloids, unless it's for some

under-the-radar good deed, like visiting a children's hospital or buying all the stunt doubles on his latest movie set a motorcycle. He's not posting opinions about current events or stirring up controversy. He's quietly leading a decent life, doing decent things, as the world's coolest and most desirable movie star. He's also pretty chill. 'I'm sorry my existence is not very noble or sublime,' he said once. Relatable! Total BAE energy.

Queen Elizabeth II

The Queen is the ultimate in BAE. She's seen dozens of prime ministers come and go. She's met every celebrity. She was once shot at while riding horseback during a parade. Although it turned out all six shots were blanks, the Queen wasn't to know that at the time, and she managed to keep the horse steady and continue with the parade like a total badass. She also rarely grants interviews. Instead of blathering on to the press about her job, her opinions or what shampoo she uses, she just goes about her business running the Commonwealth and driving Land Rovers and taking care of her millions of dogs. The Queen once said that any institution, including the monarchy, must expect criticism, but she suggested it be done with 'a touch of humour, gentleness and understanding'. Which is the alpaca philosophy in a nutshell, really.

Isambard Kingdom Brunel

People who build public infrastructure are wonderful. If you've taken a train anywhere in the world, or used a protected bike lane, or spent an afternoon in a park, give a nod of thanks to the individuals and governments who created these things.

This may not seem like a very sexy entry, but civil engineer Isambard Kingdom Brunel was actually voted the second greatest Briton in a BBC poll – right behind Churchill. This is the guy who built the Great Western Railway and also the

SS *Great Britain*, at the time the largest ship in the world. He also designed Paddington station. You know, where Paddington Bear met the Browns. In the UK, it's likely you've travelled across a bridge built by Brunel. He was the Elon Musk of his generation (minus the swagger and social media accounts). Except instead of doing things to get rich, he did them for the public good. Big alpaca energy.

Dame Helen Mirren

'You can't control how other people see you or think of you. But you have to be comfortable with that.'

There's something about movie stars we feel we've known our entire lives. Actors we've grown up watching on screen. They feel like lovely friends. And Helen Mirren is the ultimate example of this. Having alpaca energy isn't about being successful or famous (although, with an Academy Award, a Tony and an Emmy she's both of those things). She just seems very cool and full of wisdom, doesn't she? Someone who'd be fun at the pub. Who'd fill your wine glass after noticing it was nearly empty. Who'd calmly take your mobile to prevent you texting someone you shouldn't. And one thing Mirren is especially good at is taking the long view. 'We're all idiots when we're young,' she says. 'We don't think we are, but we are. So we should be.'

Céline Dion

'I've never been cool – and I don't care.'

As followers of Céline (the patron saint of love ballads that will make you cry) all know, Céline is the embodiment of big alpaca energy. She's very good at what she does and she's joyful and humble while doing it. She's funny and a bit silly

An alpaca embodying some Céline energy.

and it's impossible not to like her, while respecting her lifetime of hard work and dedication to the arts and her gift for bringing happiness to the masses. She also knows that part of her success comes from her ability to maintain a bit of privacy, atop her own private little mountain. 'Keep people dreaming,' she says. 'Close the window, and make them wonder.'

'Weird Al' Yankovic

There are few people more beloved in the music industry than 'Weird Al'. After starting out in the late 70s as a bit of a novelty act with his parody songs like 'Eat It' and 'Smells Like Nirvana', his career now spans five decades and includes five Grammy awards. His 2014 album, *Mandatory Fun*, was his first number-one hit – proving alpaca peeps are always in it for the long haul, as long as they're having fun. And in genuine alpaca fashion, he always asks permission from the artist before parodying a song. 'I don't want to hurt anybody's feelings,' he says. 'I don't want to be embroiled in any nastiness. That's not how I live my life. I like everybody to be in on the joke and be happy for my success. I take pains not to burn bridges.' Spoken like a true alpaca person.

Leisure and Pleasure

'I adore simple pleasures. They are the last refuge of the complex.'

Oscar Wilde

Alpaca Fact: Alpaca fibre is flame- and water-resistant. That means even in a thunderstorm, alpacas stay pretty dry. Which probably makes for a happier, more relaxed alpaca.

Being impermeable to fire and flame and wet is an admirable quality. For the more sensitive among us, it's very easy to feel a bit battered by the elements. Maybe we're feeling low after learning a bit of terrible

Raining today but likely sunny tomorrow.
Or in a few days.

news. After an argument (in person or online). After a hard day at work or school. After someone we like doesn't message us back. So many tiny, terrible things jabbing our souls, making even the most hardy feel a bit of despair. It's ok, though, to feel a bit overwhelmed sometimes. It's ok to curl up in a ball and wait out the worst of it.

But the alpaca person is also a tough cookie. Because a resistant outer layer allows our insides to remain happier, and more relaxed. Alpaca people can survive quite a bit – and thrive, even. Because life's too short to let the world get you down for long. Think about it. Our own ancestors survived much worse. Early arranged marriages, no dishwashers or aspirin, travel by horse and carriage or stupidly slow canoes – not to mention the unspeakable atrocities experienced by basically everyone who wasn't Caucasian. Our ancestors lived through it and survived. We know they did because here we are: living proof that everyone before us was tough enough to keep going. There's something very liberating about drawing on that strength.★ About being resistant to the little daily jabs, taking the long view, knowing we're able to handle it. It isn't about ignoring our hurt, of course. Or pretending to not be hurt by something hurtful. But it's about eventually being able to rise above those jabs – observing them, noting their intent to hurt us and *choosing not to be hurt*. You've heard the phrase 'like water off a duck's back'? The goal is to be like that. Or, like water off an alpaca's forehead. Whichever image works for you.

★   Let's all give a little nod to our many ancestors, right this moment. Thanks for living your wonderful lives that we'll never know enough about. We hope you were happy. And that you stayed warm and dry.

The Perspective Poem

I'm in it to win it,
On top of the pile
I'm deep in the cause
And it's worth all my while

I walloped opponents
I screeched into view
I battled the bullshit
To create something new

But every so often
I take a step back
To examine the change
That I want to enact

And I think and reflect
On being alive
This short time on earth
What we do to survive:

We bend and we grow
We war and we fight
We all dance together
We all find our light

We're particles of joy
We're bits of bones and matter
We're relying on each other
We're one rung on the ladder

While the journey is tough,
The solution's now clear:
If we're in this together
We've nothing to fear⋆

So now we return
Down into the fray
Restored and refreshed
The dawn of a day.

⋆ Except quicksand and alligators. Those are to be feared.

Taking a break to gain a bit of perspective.
Doesn't that cloud look like it's made
of polka dots?

> **Alpaca Fact:** The Incas referred to alpaca fleece as 'the fleece of the gods' and used it as currency. Try buying a loaf of bread with a bit of alpaca fur today, though.

The alpaca philosophy doesn't care much for the trappings of wealth and fame. That's what's so lovely about it. Anyone can live a beautiful, fulfilling alpaca life, regardless of their followers, bank accounts, pretty partners, fancy travel or beautifully renovated kitchens. Those things don't reflect a person's intrinsic value. Because, as alpacas know, money is a social construct and what has value shifts with time. Indigenous nations valued intricate wampum. Tech bros value bitcoin. English citizens during the war valued cigarettes and good stockings made from real nylon. In Newfoundland, dried cod was the currency of choice for a while. The Romans used to get paid in salt, while people in China traded in bars of tea. And of course, the Incas valued alpaca fleece. Just because society agrees things are a certain way, doesn't mean they will always be so.

So what sort of value *doesn't* shift with time? The value we place on ourselves, our families and our relationships. Not very sexy, I'll admit. But richness comes in many forms. And worrying about the stuff you'll never have isn't a great use of your time on the planet. What gives you real pleasure, anyway? A text? A purple flower? That sort of grey rainy-but-sunny weather where you just know there's a rainbow near by? A patch of sun? A medium-sized dog that's been well trained? A sausage roll after a night out? A very drunk hug? These things are available to anyone. And they're also priceless.★

So if someone with a computer can invent internet money and get people to buy imaginary bits of code to put in an imaginary wallet and then assign a random value to it, the rest of us can assign value to stuff in our lives, too. Go ahead. Do it. Look in the mirror and say, 'I'm worth it'. Whatever *it* is. That's what you're worth now. Because everything in the universe is relative and reality is what we make it. Now take your hairbrush and try and buy a carton of eggs with it. You never know.

★ Except for the sausage roll.

Alpaca-approved Pastimes

- Playing marbles
- Gently sliding blades of grass from their sheaths and nibbling the secret white tips
- Underlining something in a book
- Watering a plant in a ceramic pot and listening to the sound of the soil absorbing the water
- Taking pictures; particularly of human faces
- Knitting jumpers for penguins or little caps for newborns
- Browsing the history section at an indie bookstore
- Washing a window
- Organising your slipper collection
- Rock climbing
- Watching an art-house movie in an air-conditioned cinema on a hot afternoon
- Drinking martinis with multiple olives

- Talking lovingly to a stranger's dog or a stray cat you meet on the street
- Making a cup of black tea and adding milk, then thinking about something nice while you stir it
- Snipping stray threads from an old blanket
- Returning your library books on time
- Giving a bit of change to someone who's sleeping rough
- Handwashing your undies with gentle soap
- Chatting with someone at the bus stop
- Feeding a small, delicate thing, like a baby or a koala. Or a baby koala
- Smiling at something rude

Don't bother me darling. Life is short and
we've only got a finite number of hours
to enjoy the sunshine.

Alpaca Fact: Alpacas love a bit of sunshine.
They'll often lie out in the sun until their fleeces
are hot to the touch.

Imagine burying your face in a bit of hot alpaca fur. Sometimes the world is full of nice possibilities, yes? Now down to business: this is a public service announcement about the benefits of vitamin D which is found in sunshine and also in some less fun things, like spinach. Sitting in the sunshine and getting all hot is one of life's little pleasures, especially for those of us living in climates with cold grey winters. It lifts the spirits and, because of the healthy dose of vitamin D that comes along with those rays, sunbathing is even good for your health.★ No one really knows why,† but lower levels of vitamin D have been found in people suffering from tuberculosis, some cancers, osteoporosis, rickets, Covid-19 and other

★ Wear sunscreen.
† Scientists probably know.

nasty illnesses. Higher levels of vitamin D are thought to protect against and, in some cases, prevent these issues. Many doctors now recommend a bit of vitamin D on the regular.* So next time you spot a sunbeam, get your alpaca on. There's literally nothing easier and more relaxing than lying around in the sun.

Alpaca Fact: Alpacas are naturally curious.

'Don't be an examiner, be the interested inquirer.'

Studs Terkel

Curiosity is one of the best traits you can cultivate. Otters have it. Cats and dogs have it. Little kids have it.

---

* Talk to your doctor before taking any vitamin supplements. Remember, alpaca people are seekers of knowledge and use their common sense.

They look at the world and want to know, *why*? But as we age, we tend to lose that sense of curiosity. We're told to mind our own business, to keep our heads down or to let other people be. There are loads of benefits to being curious, though. Finding out cool stuff is the most obvious one. And curiosity can help increase feelings of empathy, which is an important part of the CLIMB method. When you ask questions and learn about someone else's situation, it helps you to understand them a bit better, and that's when the empathy kicks in. It makes life a lot sweeter when every day is an opportunity to understand something new.

So be curious,★ and surround yourself with others who also have a bit of curiosity about the world. The

---

★ It's important to note there's a difference between curiosity and scepticism. Curiosity is open, warm and kind. It's an exchange. But sceptical people today seem to take pride in explaining why their view is correct, and why you shouldn't trust in anything at all. Not your fellow humans, not the people in your communities and certainly not anyone in a position of authority. These are difficult people and they deserve a bit of empathy. They've lost their trust in the world, and that's a hard thing to get back.

ones who notice a weird bird and wonder what kind it is. The ones who read an article about spy pigeons during WWI and think, I don't know enough about that – I wonder if there's a book or documentary I can look up and learn more? The ones who reliably have fun facts to tell you at a birthday party. Stuff like, did you know allied war pigeon President Wilson suffered multiple bullet wounds in mid-flight at the hands of the German army, yet still managed to deliver an urgent message requesting artillery support for his unit? Those sorts of people. Delightful!

Alpaca Fact: Actor Nicole Kidman has a bunch of pet alpacas that live on her Australian farm.

'Everybody gets so much information all day long that they lose their common sense.'

Gertrude Stein

Sometimes a fun fact is just that. There's nothing to be learned from this. Just file it away as something entertaining to impart at your next cocktail party. You can also say stuff like, 'Did you know the unicorn is the official animal of Scotland? Or that the length of your foot is the same as your forearm?'

Alpaca Fact: Alpacas have little soft pads on their feet bottoms. No hooves here!

Unlike the clompy clump of horse hooves or the skittering scritch of the dog claw, alpacas are free to pad about the world without making too much noise.

This doesn't mean they're sneaky. But being quiet and soft-spoken can have its advantages, despite what we've been conditioned to believe: that speed, strength and aggression are essential to an animal's survival, for example; or that instilling fear via intimidation is the only way to earn respect or gain power. Alpacas, however, have survived as a species despite being gentle, accommodating and easy-going. And the alpaca commands respect despite its dopey little head and furry body and silly, soft padded feet.

So how is it possible that the alpaca has thrived while being the opposite of what a successful, powerful animal should be? The same way alpaca people thrive: by being chill, good at compromise and playing the long game. Alpaca people tend to have what's called soft power. And it's very effective. They also tend to have fewer enemies. And lower blood pressure, probably. Plus, they're more fun at parties because they listen well and won't make a scene.

Alpaca fact: Alpaca fleece is hypoallergenic. Unlike sheep fleece, it's lanolin-free. It causes offence to no one and is wearable by everyone. If alpaca fleece was a brownie, it would be a vegan brownie that still tasted good.

So next time you read a loud headline about a shark or giant-hornet type of person, remember what's going on behind the scenes. Hundreds of millions of alpaca people, staying out of danger, doing their thing, exerting their soft power in mysterious, effective ways. Like mailing you a banana bread before asking you for a favour.

The idea of something that appeals to everyone may seem like a foreign concept these days. Apart from babies, the adorableness of which most people can agree on, everyone seems polarised about everything. Extremism rules. Nuanced analysis is seen as boring or wishy-washy. 'Take a side', people shout, often impolitely. This black and white way of looking at the world is also called 'splitting' (if you're in a therapist's office). And it leads to division and heart-ache. Which is why the world needs alpacas and the alpaca philosophy more than ever.

Alpacas know that grey areas are very useful. Being undecided about something is fine.* Nuance is great, and so is compromise. They are to be cultivated and celebrated. They're the sign of someone who's a bit flexible. In fact, they are a sign of advanced moral development.

American 20th-century psychologist Lawrence Kohlberg believed there were six phases of moral development. The earlier ones were more rigid and often seen in children: stealing is bad, being nice to people is good – that sort of thing. Some people, the 'splitters', never leave this stage. But what if you're stealing bread to feed your family? Most people with a bit of empathy might admit that in this instance stealing was ok. Suddenly, they're in a higher phase of

---

* Not while driving. Driving you must pick a side. Unless you're on one of those one-track roads on the Isle of Mull, in which case middle of the road is indeed safest. See? Nothing is ever black and white.

development. A person in the sixth and highest phase uses abstract reasoning based on universal ethical principles. For example, a stage-six individual might imagine what they would do in another person's shoes – *if they believed what that other person imagined to be true*, then they'd act accordingly. Wild, right? The good news is, we actually become more nuanced as we get older, according to Kohlberg's observations. So if you're 100 per cent certain about something now, wait a few years.★ You never know what might change. You'll still be into your alpaca sweater, though. It's just so comfortable.

★   This applies to partners, too. Not to be a giant bummer, but you're likely not going to marry your first love, and that's a very good thing. You'll see.

A Very Alpaca
Reading List

Alpacas love books that take the long view. Books that have stood the test of time – that have been read all over the world in all kinds of languages for years and years. And they love stories that give us a bit of perspective about things like, well, the universe and our place in it. Alpacas also love books that are a bit weird – because alpacas appreciate weird things.

To the Lighthouse by Virginia Woolf

'One of the signs of passing youth is the birth of a sense of fellowship with other human beings as we take our place among them,' says Woolf, in a very alpaca fashion. Anyway, this is a novel about a family deciding whether to go to the lighthouse or not. It's about the rhythms of life, of the ocean, of the world and our families. Nothing much happens except life. And that's what the alpaca philosophy is all about.

One Hundred Years of Solitude **by Gabriel García Márquez**
A story that spans a hundred years and includes a family tree at the beginning. Good luck keeping track of all the characters. A classic alpaca read.

The Brilliant & Forever **by Kevin MacNeil**
This is about a literary festival on a remote Scottish island, where everyone aspires to be a writer – including the island's talking alpacas. Weird!

The Magic Mountain **by Thomas Mann**
Basically, a young man with tuberculosis spends years at a sanatorium in the Swiss Alps for about 700 pages. As anyone who's ever been unwell can attest, illness can warp our perception of time and make us re-evaluate what's important. Alpacas also love books set in the mountains.

The Pure and the Impure **by Colette**

French writer Colette wrote this novel-in-conversation about sex, gender and other stuff back in 1932. Upon its publication, a critic for the *New York Times* wrote, 'The effect of the book, on the whole, is rather empty. Except as a collection of anecdotes of uneven quality, it lacks excuse for being.' Now the book and its author are still famous and the critic long forgotten. A great reminder to take the long view.

Man's Search for Meaning **by Viktor E. Frankl**

Frankl survived the Holocaust and later wrote this memoir about his time in various concentration camps. He observed that thinking about the future helped him to avoid despair. This is a very famous book about the triumph of the human spirit in the face of incalculable cruelties.

The Year of Magical Thinking **by Joan Didion**

In order to gain perspective about what matters in life, it's useful to know how it all ends – and this is the memoir to help explain it. It is about death and loss, which may seem a bit grim, but there's nothing more invigorating than a book that makes you count your blessings. Or feel less alone in your time of grief. These are universal experiences, so why not know a bit more about them?

Work and School

*'The paradox of education is precisely this –
that as one begins to become conscious one
begins to examine the society in which he
is being educated.'*

James Baldwin

Alpaca Fact: Alpaca fur is very versatile and has
been used by the Incas for thousands of years to
create textiles of all kinds – warm woven blankets,
knitted scarves and hats, fuzzy socks to wear when
your feet are chilly. The fur is prized for its high
quality. It's also hypoallergenic and less itchy
than wool.

Alpacas 'work' in a way that maximises their usefulness to others but doesn't require a lot of effort on their part. Sounds great, doesn't it? Rather than labouring under the hot sun like a donkey or giving up their earthly bodies for human consumption like the poor chicken, alpacas have found a happy middle ground: every so often they stand around while someone else shaves their bits, and when their fur has all gone, that's it. They're done. With nothing left to give, they're free to go about their day. What they have, essentially, is built-in work boundaries. Alpacas are productive members of society with a happy work–life balance.

The alpaca philosophy is about acknowledging how much we have to give, and not stressing about the rest. This often means setting boundaries – avoiding working late hours, volunteering for projects we're not realistically able to handle, churning out shoddy work because we're already overworked; generally, doing our best at the stuff we're good at and letting the rest go. A 2019 study from ADP found that two-thirds of UK employees are overworking by an average of 6.3 hours per week, while 1 in 5 works 10 extra hours per week. That's work no one gets paid for (well, besides your employer, who's getting free labour) and it's time better spent elsewhere. Determine what you're willing to give, and then give that much. Start by clocking out at 5 pm.

Alpaca Fact: When alpacas give birth, they do it standing up. Labour usually lasts about 30 minutes. Easy, right? They're also pregnant for almost an entire year.

The length of an alpaca pregnancy is a good reminder that what we see online (adorable baby alpaca) is the end result of a buttload of effort. Look at how easily they give birth, these alpacas, we think. So efficient! But what we don't see is the year-long odyssey that led up to that moment. Which makes sense. Because no one wants to listen to an alpaca complain about how annoying it is to still be pregnant. The slog just isn't sexy. But it's good to remember that the success stories we read about tend to erase the boring bits, the failures, the bankruptcies, the down days and hours of practice and complaining that went before. Success today often appears effortless. There's even a word for it: *sprezzatura*. Originating from Baldassare Castiglione's *The Book of the Courtier* in the 16th century, this Italian word means 'a certain nonchalance, so as to conceal all art and make whatever one does or says appear to be without effort and almost without any thought about it'. But the alpaca philosophy remembers that success – our own or someone else's – isn't instantaneous. A large part of it is toiling away in obscurity. Which the alpaca person is happy to do. Eventually, they'll have a baby alpaca for their efforts.*

Alpaca Fact: Alpacas have been known to 'pronk'. This is when they use all four legs to push off the ground quickly. It's a bouncy little jump into the air that also looks very cute.

* More likely, good grades or something else less nonsensical.

Pronk is an Afrikaans word meaning to show off, strut or prance. While alpacas are generally very chill animals, they also know when it's time for a bit of pronking. The alpaca philosophy acknowledges that taking a moment, when you feel so inclined, to show off and prance around is totally cool. For some people, pronking comes naturally – hello, influencers. But for others, the ability to strut and flaunt their accomplishments can feel a little showy. The thought of drawing attention to ourselves can be a bit overwhelming and anxiety-inducing. But everyone deserves to show off their achievements every once in a while. Even if it's just a new pair of shoelaces or a bunch of muffins you didn't burn. Perhaps it's an article you wrote or a project you turned in on time.★ Remember, this isn't about a narcissistic sort of peacocking – doing something purely for attention. It's about acknowledging that at this very moment, you've done something and it feels good. And so you'd like to share your joy with others. Even if it's just your mum or bestie. So pronk away, alpaca peeps! And rest assured, you look adorable doing it.

★   Pronking a bit at work is always a good idea.

That's enough pronking for one day.
Now to sit and have a chat with these plants.

Alpaca Fact: Clothing made from alpaca fibre is extremely valuable and generally costs more than cashmere.

Alpacas know what they have to offer the world is extremely valuable. They don't sell themselves short. If an alpaca was a businessperson wearing a cute little suit, it would always get the raise. Knowing our own value isn't something that comes naturally to many, however. Some of us have grown up battling feelings of worthlessness or shame or inadequacy. Feeling like we don't measure up. Like we can't do anything right. Or maybe we feel we're not stylish enough. Not educated enough. Not accomplished enough. Even if we're lucky to be a confident sort of person, insecurities can still get us down from time to time. These feelings are all very natural.

But getting compensated appropriately for your work isn't just essential for survival, it's also a handy life skill to learn. Remember, your boss isn't doing you a favour by giving you a salary or pay cheque.

That's money★ you earned. How to get a raise? There's no big secret. Use your common sense. Ask after you've pulled off something significant. Outline your achievements and why you deserve it. Talk about what you're looking forward to accomplishing in the future. Do it in person and not via text after a bit of wine. Rehearse what you're going to say. Then ask for your raise. This works for other stuff, too. So ask for an apology. Ask for an explanation. Ask for more sprinkles. Once you know your worth, the world's your oyster.

Alpaca Fact: Unlike famous internet dogs and cats, individual alpacas have a more low-key presence online. This is partly because they're herd animals and partly because they've got better things to do.

★ If you work at a brewery, you often get paid in beer. Near where I grew up, the local brewery offered a case of beer with every pay cheque. They never had staffing issues.

For every French bulldog that has 1.2 million followers, every CEO with a bestselling book about being successful and every celebrity selling perfume with notes of kiwi fruit, bergamot and smoky tuberose, there are billions of regular folks who live quietly, offline, out of the public eye. Rather than being outspoken about their beliefs, their careers, their workout regimen, they toil away behind the scenes, happy to let the results speak for themselves. These private citizens nevertheless produce great things. You may be one of them.

Maybe you're busy serving food to people who are hungry. Maybe you're working retail and helping people pick out a new kitchen knife or some trendy gin. Maybe you're managing a team of people who depend on you at a car wash or soybean farm. Or perhaps you're taking care of birds that flew into windmills for the local bird sanctuary. Maybe you're taking care of a sibling, a parent or yourself. Perhaps you're a full-time parent. You're doing all of this work out of the public eye, with no big parade to thank you for your efforts. No one's writing articles about what a great job you're doing. It may all feel a bit

**Contributing to society by
nibbling some grass.**

thankless, sometimes. But take comfort in the idea that you're part of the silent majority: a citizen of the world, in the early days of the 21st century, toiling away with the rest of humanity, working towards something great. A vacation. A haircut. A nice meal. A chance to feel like you belong.

If you can find satisfaction in your work, it will make you a bit happier, too. A study called 'On the meaning of work: A theoretical integration and review' discovered that finding meaning in one's work increases feelings of motivation, empowerment, satisfaction and fulfilment. It also leads to decreased levels of stress. So while fame and fortune may not be on the cards for any of us, a life of satisfaction is certainly possible. If you think like an alpaca, that is.

Alpaca Fact: Just like dog and cat shows, there are alpaca shows. The British Alpaca Society, for example, puts on the BAS National Show where breeders from all over Europe and the Americas bring their best and brightest together in competition.

Look at that adorable docile animal being led in a circle around a convention hall, you might say. *I'm nothing like that*. But in fact, we're all docile animals at some point in our lives, and there's nothing wrong with that. Plodding around in a circle at someone else's direction can actually give you time to think, *Now that I've mastered this, what next?*

Throughout your lifetime there are times when you'll be asked to perform. Often you may not feel like it but being part of a performance (and being judged on it) is part of life. Generally, this starts in school, continues when you get a job and ends when you're old enough that you don't care about stuff any more. An alpaca person doesn't mind a bit of performance, though. They also don't mind if they come in last. And if they happen to come in first, that's nice too.* Participating in some kind of system – whether that's school, a club, a team or a job – is a chance to show off what you know, maybe get some fresh air and gain the kind of life experience that comes from being under a bit of pressure and doing a good job anyway.

---

* Alpaca people often do – much to the surprise of everyone who's underestimated them.

Quiz

What's your alpaca dream job?

Alpaca people don't always gravitate to the showiest jobs – they tend to get a lot of value and satisfaction out of whatever … well, whatever gives them value and satisfaction. That's just the alpaca way. Find out your alpaca dream job with the following quiz.

When it comes to what interests you, you could talk for hours about:

A. The nature of reality.

B. Latte art, sushi and lemon wheels.

C. The best roots for boiling tea.

D. The benefits of good infrastructure and your new bike.

E. Platelets, saline drips and all-inclusive vacations.

The country motto that appeals to you the most is:

A. Forward, upward, onward together (Bahamas).

B. John is his name (Puerto Rico).

C. No friend but the mountains (Kurdistan).

D. Peace, order and good government (Canada).

E. Live and work for the benefit of all mankind (South Korea).

Which essential items appear on your shopping list?

A. Headphones and energy drinks.

B. Blueberries, oat milk and greeting cards.

C. Sunscreen and granola bars.

D. Vitamin D and a book by J. G. Ballard or Jane Jacobs.

E. Ground coffee, comfortable shoes and a case of wine.

If you had to work for someone else, the ideal boss would be:

A. Someone who likes to break the rules a bit and who is self-taught in their field.

B. A people person who also loves baking their own bread.

C. You only answer to the wind; not because you're a jerk who doesn't get along with people – you just prefer to be outside in the wilderness.

D. Someone with a level of education higher than yourself who also has years of experience; someone you respect.

E. Anyone who can get the job done.

Answers

Mostly As: Computer coder. You enjoy the interconnectedness of computer systems, you love computer code and find bits and bytes and screens to be very swell. You enjoy a life that makes sense. A life of order.

Mostly Bs: Barista. You're a chill people person. You love the low-stakes vibe of working in a coffee shop, but creating delicious drinks brings you a lot of pleasure. Latte art is amazing. And you thrive on casual chit-chat with your regulars. Making connections is what drives you.

Mostly Cs: Machu Picchu guide. Life is an adventure and meant to be lived in the sun. You love helping people reach their destination and sharing your knowledge. And the mountains are pretty beautiful, too.

Mostly Ds: Tunnel engineer. While everyone is busy racing around overhead, you're way underground, calculating angles and widths and other stuff that will make us all safe and able – eventually – to zip around underground together. Thanks to a bit of government investment, some good schooling and a lot of dedication, people like you are making the world a better place.

Mostly Es: Nurse. One of humanity's greatest assets. A person who dedicates themselves to helping others. Who puts themselves in harm's way to make the world a better place. This is a job for a kind, caring person – someone who cares about civilisation, as all the best alpaca people do.

Home and the Universe

'Oh, these vast, calm, measureless mountain days,
days in whose light everything seems equally
divine, opening a thousand windows to
show us God.'

John Muir

'Never doubt that a small group of thoughtful,
committed citizens can change the world; indeed,
it's the only thing that ever has.'

Margaret Mead

Alpaca Fact: When alpacas eat grass, they bite the tips and leave the roots. They make great lawnmowers.

Alpacas understand sustainability. When they use a resource, they don't destroy it. They take what they need and allow for regrowth. This symbiotic relationship allows both the alpaca and the grass to flourish. It's something we can all learn from.

We're raised around so much excess that it's often difficult to notice it – and how complicit we are, too: we drive on big highways in big cars to big box stores where we purchase large portions of food created in a factory overseas somewhere. It seems like modern life is designed for maximum excess. Luckily, though, we have options. There are things we can do, little day-to-day bits of good, in our own little sphere of influence, to make our lives more sustainable. Avoid single-use plastics, of course. Eat a bit less meat. Walk and cycle whenever we can. Join committees and volunteer in our communities to meet like-minded

Nothing we'd rather be doing than changing the world together, one blade of grass at a time.

folks. Doing the small things we believe in on a personal level is all we can ever do. Unless, of course, you run for office, which is a noble thing to do. Start with your city council and work your way up from there. Alpacas would vote for you.

Alpaca Fact: Alpacas use a communal bathroom. The technical term is 'faeces pile'. Because alpacas prefer to go in the same spot each time, they're easily house-trained.

'Few things are brought to a successful issue by impetuous desire, but most by calm and prudent forethought.'

Thucydides

In the wild, a herd of alpacas will all somehow agree to use the same spot to do their business. Domesticated alpacas are the same. Wild, right? And also very civilised. And while it may seem a bit of a stretch to use this fact in application to our daily lives, bear with me. Civilisation exists because we all accept certain things to be true and good. Breaking the law is, for the most part, bad and should be met with consequences (civil disobedience notwithstanding; the alpaca philosophy is all about embracing the grey areas, after all). People should be courteous to one another. Books and libraries are valuable and should be funded accordingly. We should treat animals and the environment with the respect they deserve. And once we've all agreed that these basic things are good, and that they benefit all of us, for the most part, we do them. The alpaca philosophy is about doing the civilised and courteous thing. No one wants to step in errant poop. Go poop in the pile with the rest of society! And marvel at the wonders of the universe. From little bacteria and amoebae and cosmic dust – out of this chaos, we've created an imperfect but organised world with governments and political systems and communities that look out for one another. A world where human lives are valuable and good, caring people open doors for each other and pass laws about bike lanes and public housing and plant trees that won't be fully grown until we're all dead. The world is a pretty neat place.

Alpaca Fact: Baby alpacas are called crias; cria means 'baby' in Spanish.

'To have a second language, is to possess a second soul.'

Charlemagne

Alpacas are multilingual, probably, as a result of centuries of colonialism and also their peaceful co-existence with people from all over the world. Which puts them in good company. It's estimated

Cansada y disfrutando de una siesta reparadora.

that between 60 and 75 per cent of the world's population speaks more than one language. Many countries even have two or three official languages: Singapore has four and South Africa has 11, for example. That's a lot of people with impressive language skills! Being multilingual has some well-documented advantages. For example, bilingual people develop symptoms of Alzheimer's around five years later than their monolingual counterparts. (It's thought the reason for this is that the brain gets a bit of exercise switching between languages, keeping it nimble.) Multilinguals also score higher in tests measuring cultural sensitivity and open-mindedness; it appears learning new words in order to better communicate with others makes you a more sensitive person. Who knew? Alpacas, probably.

If you're one of the monolingual minority, though, it's all good, too. Nobody can help the circumstances that led to them becoming a one-language sort of human. But if you're interested in learning more (and as an alpaca person, I know you are), there's an app for that. Learning another language can be as simple as completing a few online exercises a day with a modest goal of, say, being able to read a menu in another language. Then, next time you visit Italy, you can order the cacio e pepe with confidence.

> **Alpaca Fact:** Giant ancient camels used to roam the Arctic. This is not directly alpaca related* – but it's pretty cool, don't you think?

Arctic camels used to hang out in northern Canada, much to the surprise of scientists who found a bunch of giant camel bone fragments there recently. It's thought they were about 30 per cent larger than the camels we see today. Researchers have pointed out that camels have a lot of traits that would be helpful in the great white north – humps for fat storage and big cloven feet for walking on snow. That probably came as a surprise to the camels. Surely when they arrived up north they were like, *Oh, no thank you. We're built for grassy plains and warmer weather. We must*

---

* Alpacas and camels do share ancestry.

Alpacas are resilient animals that make the best of things. Even snowy weather and hats that expose their ears.

have taken a wrong turn at the gas station. Yet they perse-vered and adapted. Like the Arctic camel, alpacas have adapted and learned to thrive in very extreme temperatures and conditions. And you can, too.

The alpaca philosophy is all about blooming where you're planted. Or, to use another cliché, doing the best with what you've got. Circumstances may never be quite right. Not all of us get to live in big cities with hotshot jobs. We don't all get to vacation in warm places and take it easy. Not everyone is in good health. We don't all get to make the choices we might have made in a perfect world, due to finances, obligations or other bummer stuff. Luckily, alpaca people are wonderful at doing well wherever they end up. Inhospitable northern climate? No problem. Crap boss? It happens. So next time you're frustrated over your circumstances, just repeat this mantra: I am a giant Arctic camel. I have the resources I need to survive and thrive.

A Note on Endings

*'Old age, calm, expanded, broad with the
haughty breadth of the universe, old age flowing
free with the delicious near-by freedom of death.'*

Edith Wharton

Alpaca Fact: Alpacas can live up to 20 years and
beyond. They're considered 'aged' at approximately
12 years and often develop arthritis, dental and
digestive issues around this time. Alpacas!
They're just like us!

In a world that feels like it caters to the young and healthy, it can be tough to get older. A bit of sag here. A few grey hairs there. But get older we must. And the alpaca philosophy is all about adapting. And embracing whatever age we are, knowing that it's often our outlook, not our chronological age, that makes us feel young or old.★

A Dutch study published in 2020 in the journal *Gerontologist* interviewed older citizens about their attitudes towards ageing and found a common theme – optimism and positivity. 'I simply still feel 20,' said one content 68-year-old man. 'I do things that a young person also does. I do not really see myself as an old person. And I hope that I can keep this feeling until I am 100.' As we age, 'we become more adaptable and flexible, and have a greater understanding of our own resilience', says US clinical psychologist Forrest Scogin. In fact, rates of depression in both men and women tend to fall after the age of 45.

★   Also, our joints, honestly. Our aching joints. Can someone draw me a bath, please? One benefit of getting older is that people start to do things for us. Lovely.

Live life with the confidence of a 12-year-old alpaca pronking over a cactus.

Which basically means everything is all good. Enjoy the age you're at. You'll never be this young again. And don't ever let anyone tell you you're old. Age is just a number and numbers are all theoretical, anyway.

Remember, just like a lively 12-year-old alpaca that's still busy pronking and eating grass: you're only as old as you feel.

In Conclusion: Alpacas Never Say Goodbye

They know they'll see you again sometime. And if not, that's also cool. Life is short. Keep calm and carry on. And always remember to enjoy the view. Because the fact is, the world is better than it's ever been before. This is very general, of course. Some places *are* worse. But overall, thanks to modern medicine, technology and progressive policies protecting our most vulnerable populations, we are better off today than at any point in human history. We have more access to clean water, technology and education than our ancestors ever did. On the whole, we live longer, healthier lives. So if you're wondering why everything feels worse, more helpless, more dysfunctional, take a breath or two. If you don't know where to turn, how to make a difference, how to operate in a world where there are so many short-term

I'm very honoured to have met you,
lovely reader. Come back soon.

distractions, how to quell the rage, how to take a step back and gain some perspective, how to move forward with hope and enlightenment … just remember: no one has any idea, really. But books can help. Hopefully, this one did the trick. And perhaps you learned something about alpacas. So if you find yourself struggling or in need of a bit of enlightenment, just remember to CLIMB. Or have a nap. That works, too.

Acknowledgments

Many thanks to my agent, Euan Thorneycroft, and to HarperCollins editorial director, Lydia Good. Thanks to Clare Faulkner for the brilliant illustrations. And many thanks to my editor Harriet Dobson and the wonderful team at HarperCollins – my copy-editor Anne Newman, the proofreaders, production team, marketing, publicity and sales – and to every bookseller and librarian who helps make books like this a success.

About the Author

Jennifer McCartney is a *New York Times* bestselling author. She is the author of *The Little Book of Sloth Philosophy* and *The Little Book of Otter Philosophy*. She has also written *The Joy of Leaving Your Sh★t All Over the Place*, *Cocktails for Drinkers*, *Poetry from Scratch* and the novel *Afloat*. Her work has appeared in the *Atlantic*, *Vice* magazine, *Teen Vogue*, *Architectural Digest*, *Backpacker* magazine and many other publications. She also writes regularly for *Publishers Weekly*. Like the alpaca, she plays well with others, is a bit furry overall and generally stays out of trouble.

HarperCollins*Publishers*
1 London Bridge Street
London SE1 9GF

www.harpercollins.co.uk

First published by HarperCollins*Publishers* in 2020

1 3 5 7 9 10 8 6 4 2

Text and poetry © Jennifer McCartney 2020
Illustrations © Clare Faulkner 2020
All poetry is the author's own unless otherwise stated

Jennifer McCartney asserts the moral right to
be identified as the author of this work

A catalogue record of this book is
available from the British Library

HB ISBN 978-0-00-839274-1
EB ISBN 978-0-00-839257-4

Printed and bound in Great Britain by
CPI Group (UK) Ltd, Croydon

MIX
Paper from
responsible sources
FSC™ C007454

This book is produced from independently certified FSC™ paper
to ensure responsible forest management.

For more information visit: www.harpercollins.co.uk/green